The Solar System

Exploring

SPACE

Ashley Lee

Explore other books at:
WWW.ENGAGEBOOKS.COM

VANCOUVER, B.C.

WWW.ENGAGEBOOKS.COM

The Solar System: Level 1
Lee, Ashley 1995 –
Text © 2020 Engage Books

Edited by: A.R. Roumanis
and Jared Siemens

Text set in Arial Regular.
Chapter headings set in Arial Black.

FIRST EDITION / FIRST PRINTING

LIBRARY AND ARCHIVES CANADA CATALOGUING IN PUBLICATION

Title: The Solar System Level 1
Names: Lee, Ashley, author.

Identifiers: Canadiana (print) 20200309765 | Canadiana (ebook) 20200309773
ISBN 978-1-77437-707-9 (hardcover)
ISBN 978-1-77437-708-6 (softcover)
ISBN 978-1-77437-709-3 (pdf)
ISBN 978-1-77437-710-9 (epub)
ISBN 978-1-77437-711-6 (kindle)

Subjects:
LCSH: Solar system—Juvenile literature

Classification: LCC QB501.3 .L44 2020 | DDC J523.2—DC23

Contents

What Is the Sun?

The Sun is a star.
Stars make light.
They are very hot.

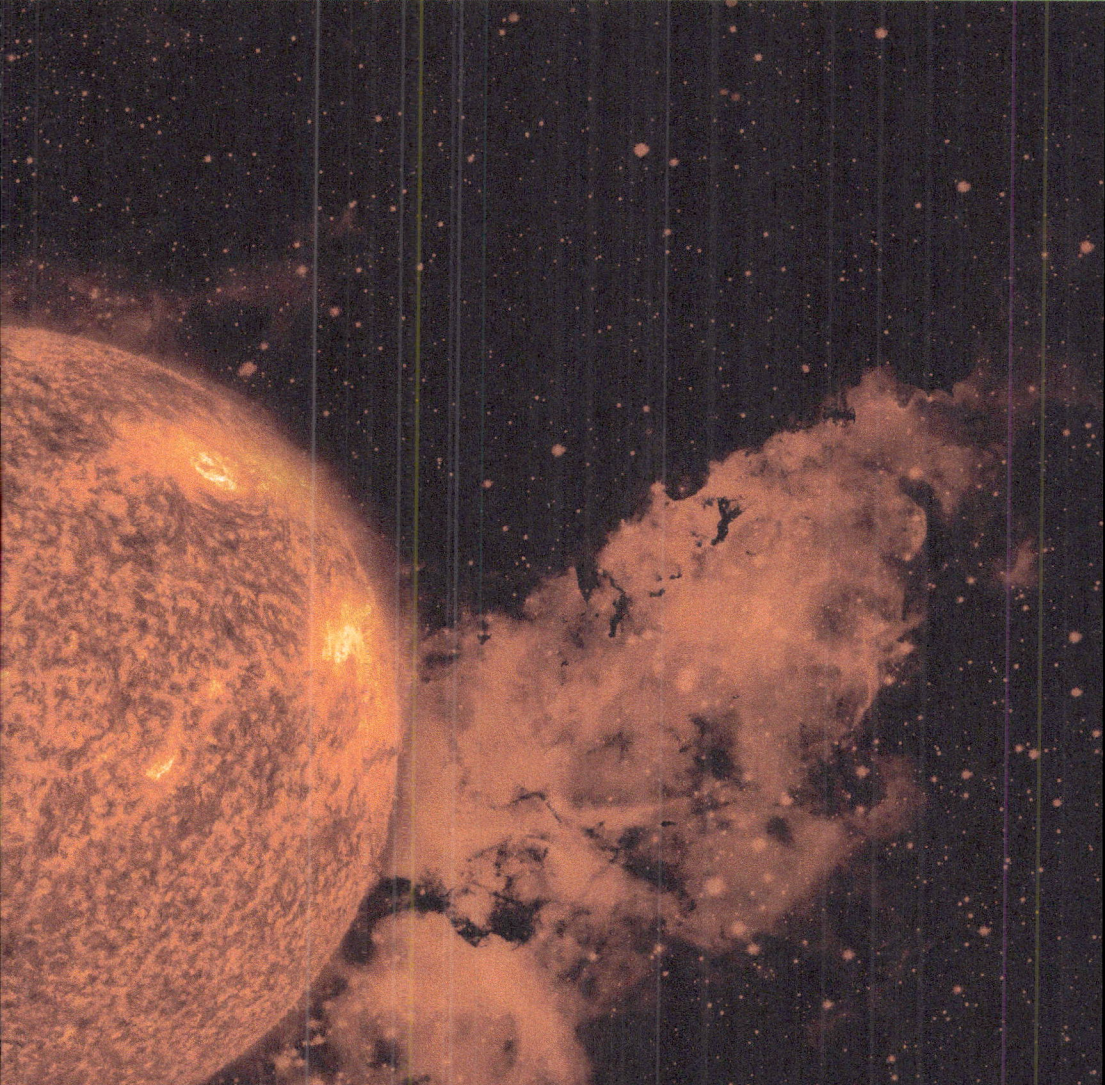

The Sun looks bigger than other stars. It looks bigger because other stars are further away.

What Is the Solar System?

The Sun is at the center of the solar system.

All things that move
around the Sun are part
of the solar system.

What Are Planets?

A planet is a round object that moves around a star.

Mercury Venus Earth Mars

Jupiter

Saturn

Uranus

Neptune

There are eight planets
in the solar system.

What Is Mercury?

Mercury is the smallest planet. It is also the closest planet to the Sun.

What Is Venus?

Venus is the hottest planet. It has many mountains and volcanoes.

What Is Earth?

Earth is the only planet in the solar system known to support life. It has oceans that make the planet look blue.

What Is Mars?

Mars is a red planet.
Just like Earth, Mars
has changing seasons.

What Is Jupiter?

Jupiter is the largest planet. It has about 80 moons.

What Is Saturn?

Saturn has about seven main groups of rings. These rings are made out of ice and rock.

What Is Uranus?

Uranus is the coldest planet. It is called an ice giant because it is mostly made up of ice.

What Is Neptune?

Neptune is the furthest planet from the Sun.

The winds on Neptune are some of the strongest in the solar system.

What are Dwarf Planets?

Dwarf planets are round objects that circle the Sun. They share their space with other objects. The solar system has five known dwarf planets.

Haumea spins about six times faster than Earth.

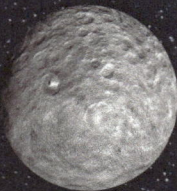

Ceres is the smallest dwarf planet.

Makemake takes 309 years to travel around the Sun.

Eris is the farthest planet from the Sun.

Pluto is the largest dwarf planet.

What Is the Moon?

The Moon travels around Earth. The Moon is about four times smaller than Earth.

A spacecraft is needed to get to the Moon. Spacecraft carry people and tools into space.

What Is an Astronaut?

An astronaut is a person who travels to space.

In 1969, Neil Armstrong became the first person to walk on the Moon.

Exploring Space

People sometimes send robots to explore space. Robots can explore areas of space that are difficult for humans to reach.

A robot called *Curiosity* has been exploring Mars since 2012. *Curiosity* is looking for signs of life on Mars.

Living on Mars

People hope to one day build a city on Mars. Living on Mars would allow scientists to better study the solar system.

Large spacecraft are being built by a company called SpaceX. A trip to Mars would take about 6 months in one of these spacecraft.

Life Beyond Earth

Sometimes, animals on Earth become extinct. This means there are no more of them left.

Exploring space can help humans find new homes. Bringing animals to these places can help make sure that they do not go extinct.

29

Quiz

Test your knowledge of the solar system by answering the following questions. The questions are based on what you have read in this book. The answers are listed on the bottom of the next page.

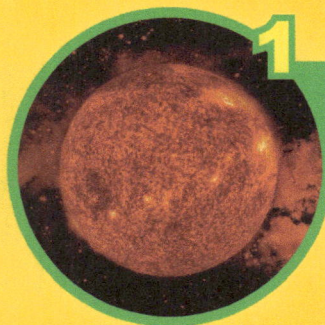

1 What is at the center of the solar system?

2 What shape are planets?

3 How many planets are in the solar system?

4 What is the name of the planet that is closest to the Sun?

5 What is the name of the largest planet in the solar system?

6 How many known dwarf planets are in the solar system?

Explore other Level 1 readers!

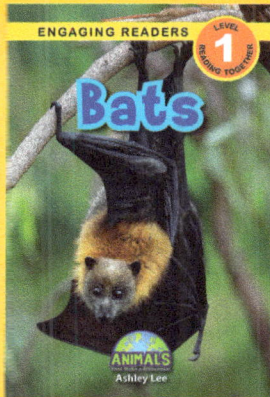

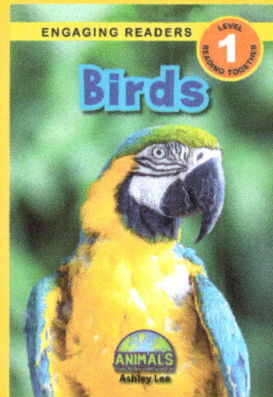

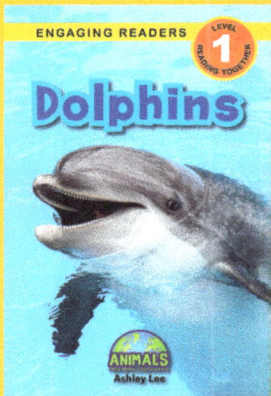

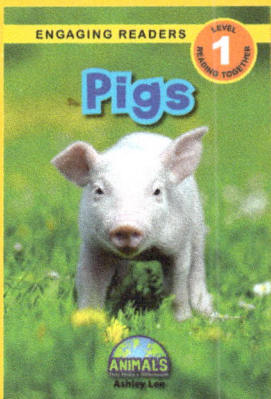

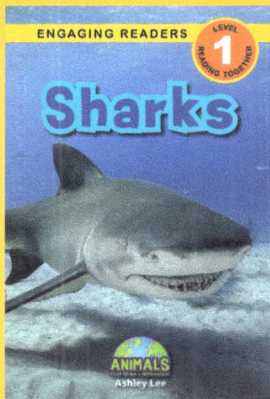

Visit www.engagebooks.com to explore more Engaging Readers.

www.ingramcontent.com/pod-product-compliance
Lightning Source LLC
Chambersburg PA
CBHW040850030426

R18075000001B/R180750PG42331CBX00002B/3

9 781774 377086